PSALM 91

THE MYSTERY OF THE SECRET PLACE OF THE MOST HIGH

HOW TO TRUST GOD FOR DIVINE PROTECTION

GOD HAS MORE IN STORE FOR YOU THAN YOU CAN EVER IMAGINE!!!

A study of one of the most interesting and impactful Psalms of the Holy Bible. There are thousands of mysteries stored in this seemingly simple Psalm. Is your mind open enough and prepared to receive God's promise in a fresh way?

God is a loving father, a merciful God and also a calm spirit. There is this other part of him that Christians tend to ignore or forget: That he is also a raging fire, a man of war. It is this part of his personality that this book is going to be revealing to you.

If there is one thing I want to assure as a friend of God, it is that God wants to protect you but the Devil will do everything in his power to try to make you miss out on it. Learn how to outwit him and his cohorts forever and ever. Amen!

Preface

If there is one thing the Devil is very good at, it is persistence. He is very persistent in his efforts to take down the sons of God and get them to doubt their father and his ability to protect them.

In my years of Christianity, I have come across a number of Christians who have confessed to seeking protection from false Gods simply because they have been convinced by the Devil that God cannot protect them. In the end, that is only a trap to deceive them and drag them back into the hand of the Devil and his cohorts. Seeking for protection from the Devil is a vain effort, because it is the Devil who is trying to hurt you. Running back to him is like running into a lion's Den when been chased by a lion.

Unfortunately, many Christians fall into this trap because they don't know how to claim their portion of God's promise of protection from the Bible. One of such vivid scriptures where such a promise is clearly written out is in the book of Psalm, in its 91st chapter. That is why I decided to write this book: to help my fellow Christians understand how to claim God's promises in this verses.

Follow me prayerfully on this adventure of God's word. Stay blessed.

TABLE OF CONTENTS

BRIEF HISTORY OF PSALM 91

THE SECRET PLACE OF THE MOST HIGH AND THE SHADOW OF THE ALMIGHTY

Who will be protected in the secret place of the most high?

Where is the secret place of the most high?

Why are God's children evicted from the secret place?

The shadow of the Almighty

THE PLACE OF TRUST IN PSALM 91

Steps to build trust and enjoy God's promises in Psalm 91

Eliminate worry from your life

Monitor your thought process

Flood your mind with God's promises from his word

Spend more time with God

Remember all of the times God has been faithful

What do you do with this?

BRIEF HISTORY OF PSALM 91

It is no news that Psalm 91 is one of the most popular Bible chapters of all time. The Psalm has been used for a lot of activities and has continued to serve its purpose for God's children even centuries after it was written. Every single chapter in the Bible is packed with its own inherent power, but Psalm 91 has proven to be very important for divine protection. Even those in the occult world have gotten a full knowledge of this psalm and how it can be used in twisted ways. So there is no reason why you, as a bona-fide child of God, shouldn't claim all the promises God has listed for you in this chapter of the psalm.

But first, before you can maximize the values inherent in anything, it is important to understand or have a small history of how that thing came to be.

How did this Psalm get into the Bible and become so important for everyday Christian living? Bible scholars will tell you there are various ways which a reader can tell the person who penned down a psalm. One of such ways is to look at its title. For example, the psalm preceding psalm 91 (psalm 90) has its title as *The Prayer of Moses* and psalm 23 is popularly referred to as *A Psalm of David.* From these two examples, it is easy to identify the people who penned down these psalms. One was Moses and the other was written by David. Bring this same bible logic into psalm 91, and we notice a flaw, which is that psalm 91 has no title, so it is hard to identify its writer. There is no way to tell the day it was written and its composition history with utmost certainty.

There are numerous unfounded speculations that point to Moses as the writer of that psalm, given that some of the idiomatic expressions used in this chapter closely resemble those from Deuteronomy, a book penned by Moses on the mountain. On the other hand, there is even more reason to believe that it was David who was inspired to document his experience in the hands of his enemies and how God saw him through it all. But in all of this, there is never enough evidence for us to get to a suitable conclusion.

Apart from this method, there is another way to know the person who penned down a psalm, and this can be done by checking to see if that particular psalm was referenced in another portion of the bible. Take Psalm 2 which goes without a title, but later appears somewhere in The book of Acts 4 vs 25 - 26. Here, this psalm is attributed to David. Going through the scriptures, there is no place that references Psalm 91 and also mentions its writer.

That being settled, we have to go back to Psalm 90, which was written by Moses. Many bible scholars have a theory that if the writer of a psalm isn't identified anywhere in the Bible, then it is safe to say that the writer of that psalm is the same as the writer of the one before it. Following this logic, we can start to believe that Moses may have penned down this psalm. But let's not jump into conclusion yet. It is too early for that.

In the 14th verse of that psalm, we can see the writer using the phrase, *Set his love upon me.* There is only one other place where something similar to that line can be found in the Bible, and that is in Deuteronomy 7 vs 7 which start this way: *The Lord did not set his love upon you....* Moses is the writer of that book of the Bible, and this further goes to support claims that he could have been the writer of that Psalm.

In the end, we are torn between two options: David or Moses. No one can say for sure which of them wrote this wonderful verse, but there is one thing that can be deduced here, which is that the writer of that Psalm had been greatly influenced by the Holy Spirit and must have had a thousand adventures while faithfully hiding under the shadow of the almighty.

THE SECRET PLACE OF THE MOST HIGH AND THE SHADOW OF THE ALMIGHTY

I love to read Psalm 91. It is an exciting adventure into one of God's best known promise. What is even better is the way it starts. The first verse of this chapter goes thus:

He that dwelleth in the secret place of the most High shall abide under the shadow of the Almighty.

Growing up as a little child, I can't tell you how many times I finished up the Bible. Of course, I did that because I loved the stories, ranging from God showcasing his power at the Red sea to the way one Angel singlehandedly slayed more than 185,000 Assyrian soldiers in one night. But on getting to the book of Psalm, I discovered something even more fascinating. This book wasn't filled with stories like the other books of the Bible, so I skipped it and went over to the Book of Proverbs. I found the Book of Proverbs more inviting than the 'abstract' Book of Psalms. I couldn't place my fingers on a reason why the writer of the Bible (For a long time I continued to think that the

Bible had been singlehandedly written by Jesus) had decided to include these boring lyrics into this perfect book. So it was a shock to me the day my mother asked me to read up Psalm 91 before going to bed one night.

I can still remember that night clearly in my head as I laid on my bed and read that first verse. These keywords struck me: *dwelleth, secret place* and *Shadow of the Almighty.* The next day I didn't go back to my stories, instead I revisited that scripture to see if I could discover anything enlightening. The word *shadow* was the one that tormented my mind the most. All my life I had been conditioned to see darkness as evil. Shadows were dark, so I wondered why the Almighty who is supposed to be an embodiment of light would have a shadow. It was mind-boggling, but there was no way I could contest this. The Holy Bible had not only stated that the Almighty had a shadow but had also gone ahead to insinuate that this shadow could act as a protection for God's children who have decided to dwell in this secret place. Little did I know at the time that the Bible was full of mystery and if you didn't ask the Holy Spirit for help with understanding it will be hard to have a full grasp of what God is trying to communicate to you.

Who will be protected in the secret place of the most high?

Before we get too excited when reading this verse of the scripture, it is important to understand who God was referring to when he inspired the writer to put down the words.

The first thing that should be noted about *the secret place of the most high* is that it is not for everyone. Unbelievers and people who have no connection with God do not have a place in this secret place. This is not to say that God is now a partial God, but his promises such as the one in question come with conditions and if these conditions are not met, the believer cannot take a full delivery of these promises. There must be a close friendship. Remember that God can protect whoever he wants to protect but this person will need to have a fellowship with him before he/she can claim this promises.

Looking at the way in which this scripture was created, one can see that it is a promise that comes in the third person present tense. The scripture did not say *He who once dwelled in* or *He that will someday dwell in*. The writer is specific in his words selection, making it open to the reader that the promise is for those who currently dwell in and who continue to dwell. This means that as long as a person continues to dwell, the promise of protection continues to manifest itself in their life. Once a disconnection occurs between the Almighty and any individual, the individual is instantly taken off the secret place and is left to the mercies of the Devil and his cohorts. But the grace abounds and there is always room for reacceptance into this stronghold of protection.

To *dwell* in this sense means to live a godly and holy life, someone who is active in the service of God and his kingdom. It is true that you can't buy God's favor and blessing, but remaining in his sanctuary and serving him continually can help secure these promises for the believer.

In the translation of the Book of Psalms, the Hebrew word **Yashab** was used to represent the English word 'dwell'. The definition of this Hebrew word literally means to sit, or to remain, or to stay, or to inhabit. It generally goes to mean existing fully in a place. From this literal translation, it is easy to see where the writer of that scripture was coming from. He wanted readers of that scripture to learn to sit with God in the study of his word and in meditation. He wanted readers to inhabit God's presence in praises, in worship and in holiness. In the presence of the Lord our God is everlasting comfort, fullness of grace and exceeding love. It is a truly wonderful place to dwell in, so why do people end up leaving to go somewhere dangerous. It is because the Devil, the chief deceiver of the brethren, is never happy to see us in the presence of our father. He is never happy to have you in a place where he cannot lay his hands on you. Look at what he told God in Job 1 vs 10, he said *Hast not thou made a hedge about him, and about his house, and about all that he hath on every side? Thou hast blessed the work of his hands and his substance is increased in the land.*

Job is a perfect example of a man who dwelled in the secret place of the most high. What is even more beautiful is the fact that this protection extended even up to his family, his cattle and on every side around him. Everything that was connected to Job was protected simply because he decided to dwell in the secret place of the most high. Anyone who has left this secret place may experience a level of success and financial stability, but in the end he/she remains a prey in the hands of the Devil and his cohorts. This people never experience true peace in their lives.

Where is the secret place of the most high?

Now that we have established the people who will be protected in the secret place, it is equally important that we establish where the secret place is and what it is.

As the name implies, the secret place is God's stronghold, a place the Devil himself cannot reach. Have you ever tried to hide something before? Either a secret from your past or money that you don't want someone to steal? Chance is very high that you have tried to hide something important and dear to you to prevent its exposure and damage. Try to remember how much you brainstormed the perfect location for hiding this precious thing. Imagine the joy you felt when you finally found the perfect place to keep it safe. If you did your job well, then nobody who isn't you will ever be able to have access to that secret thing. Same way it is with God.

The first verse of this Psalm has given us a promise of being kept safely in God's secret place, in Heaven's vault where we will be protected by all of the Angels of battle. The secret place of God is what it is, a secret place that nobody knows. The secret place is a place where God keeps his children so that even the Devil himself can't have any access to them. The secret place is a special and reserved place for the saint that only God has access to. Imagine the Devil trying to hurt you or your family and coming to earth to discover that he can't find you anywhere around, even with all of his network here on earth. Isn't that the kind of protection you want? This cannot be gotten anywhere except in the secret place of the most high.

Why are God's children evicted from the secret place?

With all of these benefits associated with the admission into the secret place, one can easily see why it isn't for everyone. Admission into the secret place of the most high must be earned. This place isn't for the lazy Christian who cannot witness to lost souls. It isn't for Christians who do not hold their Creator in high esteem and reference his presence. Considering the verse in Hebrew 4 vs 11 that says: *Let us labour therefore to enter into that rest, lest any man fall after the same example of unbelief.* This verse of the Bible makes it very open that the child of God will have to work to enjoy this promise of rest. The important word here is *labor*. God wants you experience rest in the secret place, but the Devil will do everything in his power to prevent you from enjoying this rest. It is the battle against the Devil and his cohorts preventing your progress into the secret place of rest that becomes the act of *labour*.

In your journey into the secret place, you will be faced with a lot of doubts, discouragements and disappointments. The child of God will need to equip himself with enough spiritual empowerment to break through these dark forces and access the secret place.

God is a God of discipline and justice and he is ever careful to ensure that the wrong people don't find their way into this secret place. He too dwells in the secret place, in fact, this secret place exists inside of him.

John 15 vs 4 puts it this way: *Abide in me, and I in you. As the branch cannot bear fruit of itself, except it abide in the vine; no more can ye, except ye abide in me.*

The concept of God being the secret place is a spiritual one that can only be understood by spiritual people. The natural mind cannot conceive it. Looking closely at the words used in John 15 vs 4, one can see that they closely resemble those used in Psalm 91 vs 1. Words such as abide and dwell have close interpretation. It is easy to see that this secret place of the most high is in Christ, in God and in the Holy Spirit. Being in the secret place is to have a communion with the trinity. Being in this secret place doesn't only protect you from physical harm. It goes beyond that. You are also covered and protected from spiritual harm, from the fiery darts of the enemy that fly around every day. This is why some Christians may face physical persecution but their faith in God remains strong, because their spirits and souls cannot be accessed by the Devil.

With this, it is easy to see why God cannot tolerate any form of sin or darkness from people who dwell in this secret place. You can't exist inside of God and litter his insides with darkness and filth. God, our father, is too righteous to tolerate this. It is just like a father and son enjoying a nice time in the sitting room and the son decides to release a fart. Not only is that unacceptable, it is also very disrespectful and it can secure the son an eviction from the sitting room until the smell has vanished from the air. Same way it is with God.

Sin causes eviction from God's presence, but this doesn't mean that the evicted person ceases to be a child of God. It simply means that they have been given time off to go wash themselves and present themselves to be reaccepted into the secret place before the Devil is able to find them. And this is the place where asking for forgiveness becomes important.

This is why David pleaded in Psalm 51 vs 7 where he said *Purge me with hyssop, and I shall be clean: Wash me and I shall be whiter than snow.* He goes further to say in verse 9: *Hide thy face from my sins, and blot out all mine iniquities.*

To purge something, as it is stated in scripture, means to cleanse, to get rid of a prominent and embarrassing stain. From the book of Leviticus 14 vs 6 - 7, there is instruction to the priests as regards using hyssop to cleanse a person formerly plagued by leprosy. It goes thus,

6 As for the living bird, he shall take it, and the cedar wood, and the scarlet, and the hyssop, and shall dip them and the living bird in the blood of the bird that was killed over the running water:

7 And he shall sprinkle upon him that is to be cleansed from the leprosy seven times and shall pronounce him clean, and shall let the living loose into the open field.

David penned down this verse of the Psalm when he discovered that he had done something that had displeased God. He was sure that his sin had gotten him evicted from God's presence. After experiencing God's protection for a greater part of his life, David was smart enough to understand that he needed to make his way back into God's secret place or risk getting crushed by the Devil and his machinations. With a humble spirit, David returned to God, the father and asked for forgiveness. God's forgiveness was his ticket for readmission into the secret place.

The shadow of the Almighty

Most people love to base their research on the first verse of Psalm 91 only on the promise of *the secret place*. But if you look objectively at that verse, you can easily see that there is something else there, another promise that remains to be claimed. This promise refers to the *shadow of the Almighty.*

I really love how poetic the writer of this chapter was. His choice of words amazes me. In fact, I consider Psalm 91 a poem of protection. *The shadow of the Almighty.* That phrase brings a lot of powerful pictures to mind. Briefly close your eyes and imagine yourself standing close to Mount Everest with the Sun at the other side of the mountain. Picture the large and ginormous shadow that will be casted on the ground because of this setting. I am pretty sure you can't picture it because it is more than you mind can contain. Now imagine the shadow of the ALMIGHTY. THE ALMIGHTY! THE ONE MIGHTIER THAN THE MIGHTIEST! Don't allow your mind wander too far because that cannot be imagined. But this is just to help you see a small picture of what it means to be hidden in the shadow of the almighty. He is a shadow with perimeters that the Devil dreads, perimeters that the Devil cannot cross into.

It is just like when the Sun is out in the sky in all of its fury and is burning your back with its scorching heat. The smart thing to do is to find a shade and protect your skin until it is safe to return to the road. Same way it is it with the world. This heat of darkness is burning every day and there is one place where a person can receive 'coolness', and that is under the shadow of the Almighty.

Using our example of a traveler hiding under a shadow, at some point this traveler will have to leave this shadow and continue on his journey, if not there is risk of getting home late or missing an appointment. The beautiful thing about the shadow of the almighty is that once you go into it, it becomes home. It is not a temporary resort where you will have to pay or be ejected. It is a permanent residence and the only ticket for continued inhabitation is a constant fellowship with its owner. In this shadow is continuous comfort and spiritual blessing to last you a life time.

Let's see what the Bible says about the shadow of the almighty in Exodus 13 vs 20 – 22.

²⁰ And they took their journey from Succoth, and encamped in Etham, in the edge of the wilderness.

²¹ And the LORD went before them by day in a pillar of a cloud, to lead them the way; and by night in a pillar of fire, to give them light; to go by day and night:

²² He took not away the pillar of the cloud by day, nor the pillar of fire by night, from before the people.

In this verse, we are given a picture of a group of people travelling through a wilderness. Now, you don't need to be reminded about how hot and dry wildernesses are. People drop dead from the heat while travelling through these places. God knew that his children, who were being led on their journey by Moses, would need something to shield them from the sun in the day and fire to warm them and give them light at night. He was there with them and provided these things.

Something even more intriguing about this pillar of cloud and fire that God kept for his children is that they did not only protect them from elemental harm, they also saw them through physical harm. This is why Pharaoh and his army were not able to hurt the Israelites at the Red Sea. Why? Because they were under the shadow of the Almighty. In this case the shadow of the almighty was represented by the dual pillars. For every Christian, God provides a specific shadow to cater to their needs. It doesn't always have to be a pillar. He is the all-knowing God and he knows what a person needs best in any situation.

THE PLACE OF TRUST IN PSALM 91

It is no news that the Bible, which is God's word inspired by the Holy Spirit, is filled with thousands of promises for the believer. In truth, it is one thing to have a promise made to you and it is another thing to find that promise and finally it is a totally different thing to lay hold of all of the benefits associated with that promise. As children of God, it is important that we know that God has made promises to us through his word and it is more important that we know how to access the benefits of these promises.

In the second verse of this Psalm, we are given one of the ways in which a child of God can claim the blessings of God in this Psalm.

I will say of the LORD, He is my refuge and my fortress: my God; in him will I trust.

TRUST! That is an important key word in that verse. The promise of a fortress or a refuge which closely resemble the promise of *the secret place of the most high* both hinge on the powerful string of God's word and these promises. Nothing is more important to God than trust and faith in his word. In fact, you can simply put it that faith is the sickle with which we harvest God's blessings.

From this above, it is easy to see that the writer of this Psalm fully understood the benefits associated with trust in God. It is easy to see that he had a state of mind that hopes totally on God and his promise of the refuge and fortress. This kind of trust is one that is built overtime, on a solid foundation of various experiences with God. The problem most Christians face is that they find it hard to put in their full trust in God. A fellow Christian once said to me, 'It is hard to trust someone I can't see or hear.' Instantly, I got to know that he wasn't connected in the Spirit, because trust is a spiritual virtue. People who work in the flesh do not have the foundation to build a solid trust in God, and even when they try to develop it, it comes crumbling down at the sight of one problem or another. When operating in the flesh, there is absolutely no reason why you should trust a spirit being, someone invisible. But I want you to understand that God is more real than the air you breathe or the food you eat. You only have to come to a place where you are connected enough to feel his manifestation.

For you to enjoy the promises loaded in this book of Psalms, you first have to believe that God cares for your wellbeing and is also able to protect you by placing you in his fortress. You need to trust God and his all-seeing ability, his power to identify the Devil's plans and thwart them before they come to fruition. You will need to trust God that he is all-powerful and able to fulfill his promise of protection. The problem with us in the Christendom is that most of the people who claim to be children of God do not always believe in his ability to wage war against the Devil and conquer on their behalf. We have been so taught to believe that God is a merciful and gentle God, which is very true, but God is also a God of War when he needs to be.

Let's see some prominent scriptures (old and new testament) that show God as a Man of war.

The LORD is a man of war: the LORD is his name. **Exodus 15 vs 3**

But the LORD is with me as a mighty terrible one: therefore, my persecutors shall stumble, and they shall not prevail: they shall be greatly ashamed; for they shall not prosper: their everlasting confusion shall never be forgotten. **Jeremiah 20 vs 11**

These shall make war with the Lamb, and the Lamb shall overcome them: for he is Lord of lords, and King of Kings: and they that are with him are called, and chosen, and faithful. **Revelation 17 vs 14**

These are a few of the scriptures that helped shape my perception of God as a divine warrior that will do everything to keep his children safe from the hands of the Devil. Christ has already paid the final price on the cross and that is all that matters. Even though the Devil will keep trying to see if he can get lucky, we still keep conquering him and taking all of the victory through Christ Jesus.

This trust in God and the promise of his word is something that needs to be developed if a person is to take a full delivery of the promise of this chapter of the Bible. Trust isn't something you make up your mind to give to somebody, even God. Trust is built. It is just like when we meet people in our everyday lives, we don't immediately start to trust them. It takes time and a period of interaction before we can give them all our trust. This trust is given because you can now say that you understand these people as well as you would want before entrusting anything of value into their hands. Same way it is in our relationship with God. If you don't know him enough you will never be able to trust him. Get into fellowship and friendship with God where you communicate with him every day and get to know him better through his word. His word is enough to tell you everything you need to know about him, everything about his personality, his likes and dislikes and his kingdom.

Steps to build trust and enjoy God's promises in Psalm 91

With that out of the way, then you can follow these steps to build your trust even further and receive all of the promises in Psalm 91.

Eliminate worry from your life

If you know nothing about the Devil, then please know this: one of his greatest weapon against the saint is the weapon of worry. Worrying as a child of God goes to undermine God's power and grace. Worry is a form of doubt, a way of telling God that you don't think he is capable of protecting you.

Philippians 4 vs 6 tells us: *Be careful for nothing; but in everything by prayer and supplication with thanksgiving let your requests be made known unto God.*

This verse of the scripture is more like a commandment to the child of God telling him/her not to accommodate worry but instead had over the burden to God. Unfortunately, most of us Christians never heed to this commandment, instead we prefer to hold on to our worries and anxieties and ignore God completely. In the end, all this succeed in doing is making him feel small and irrelevant and if there is one thing I know about my God, it is that he always wants to be a part of my life.

The Devil knows how much God hates worry so he will do everything to introduce it into your life. Worry takes your focus away from God and places it on your problem so much so that you lose focus of what God is capable of doing. The Devil gets excited whenever he succeeds in planting the seed of worry.

For you to enjoy the benefit of protection embedded in Psalm 91, you must make a conscious effort to trust God. Sure, there will be temptations to do otherwise, but with the help of the Holy Spirit you will be empowered to do that. Whenever you find yourself worrying about the safety of your children, spouse or loved ones, remind yourself of God's promise of protection. In fact, it has become even easier to do that in this modern age of digitalization. Worry can creep up on you while at work or during your commute. In the absence of your physical/hardcopy Bible, you can gently flip through the pages of your Bible App and reassure yourself of God's word. But when doing this, never forget that the word is not powerful because it is coming from a digital or physical platform. It is powerful because it exists in your mind as a flaming fire that will quench all the worry darts the Devil shoots your way.

Trusting God is not something that will come easy. It is an active decision that the Devil will always challenge. He will try to challenge everything you know and believe about God's promises in this Psalm. The Devil will make you worry that your kids aren't safe in school. Don't fall for his trick. You have the mind of Christ and you are destined for greater things than you can imagine, so God cannot afford to lose you to the Devil. People talk about a mind condition known as paranoia where their minds are constantly being plagued by a delusion that someone is after them. Paranoia is a mechanism used by the Devil to induce fear in the child of God and force them to worry.

Monitor your thought process

Let's start this by looking at a scripture in 2 Corinthians 10 vs 4 – 5.

4 For the weapons of our warfare are not carnal, but mighty through God to the pulling down of strong holds:

5 Casting down imaginations, and every high thing that exalteth itself against the knowledge of God, and bringing into captivity every thought to the obedience of Christ.

This is a powerful scripture that tells us about our thoughts and how God wants us to handle them. The verse says *casting down imaginations,* especially all of those imaginations that do not conform to God's word and his authority. These are the imaginations that the Devil feeds on to bring your greatest fear to fruition. If you continue entertaining those thoughts, one day he will become the chief of your mind, stirring it in any direction he wishes at any point in time.

Like has been stated before, the Devil always wages war on the mind of the brethren. Once He discovers that you have decided to start trusting God completely, he starts to wage a war. These negative thoughts that come in the form of depression, feeling of rejection and dejection are capable of creating a rift between you and your Father. The sweet thing about the Devil is that with the help of the Holy Spirit the child of God can easily study his machinations and figure a pattern or attack. Once this pattern is figured out, it becomes easier to outwit him with the wisdom of God you already have inside of you.

Flood your mind with God's promises from his word

Do you want to trust God more? Then you have to fill your mind with more of his promises to you. One major reason why the people of the world always end up with negative thoughts, is because of the things they fill their minds with. When you fill up your mind with stories of the most disastrous happenings in the word, the mind will provide you with fear at the slightest instance. But when you continue to fill your mind with godly virtues and promises, your mind will have no other choice than to feed you with faith and trust when the time comes for it. Never forget that input will always beget output.

Matthew 12 vs 34, *O generation of vipers, how can ye, being evil, speak good things? For out of the abundance of the heart the mouth speaketh.*

Philippians 4 vs 8, *Finally, brethren, whatsoever things are true, whatsoever things are honest, whatsoever things are just, whatsoever things are pure, whatsoever things are lovely, whatsoever things are of good report; if there be any virtue, and if there be any praise, think on these things.*

Imagine this exciting picture to get a clearer view of this: Think of your mind as a piece of foam. If you soak that foam into a bucket filled with blue dye and then bring it out to squeeze, there is no way you will have a red coloured liquid oozing out of the foam. It will be blue dye that will flow out. Also, if you soak that foam into a bucket of water and then squeeze, there is no way it will ooze out dye. That is just how it is with the mind. Soak your mind with bright and colorful thoughts about God's words and when it is time to squeeze, you will get back all of the colorful and godly thoughts. On the other hand, if you have soaked your mind in the disheartening news of the world, you will be fed the same when it is time.

Spend more time with God

One problem we face as Christians is that we don't spend enough time with God, our father, basking in the beauty of his presence. Not only will spending time in God's presence help you to build trust, it will also protect you more from the grip of the Devil. The Devil and his cohorts have no place in God, they cannot survive his presence except when he wills them to (as we saw in Job when the Devil came among the children of God to complain about Job).

Sit down and ask yourself if there is anything that may be taking you away from God and his presence. Is it sin? An addiction? A grudge? Whatever it may be, do everything in your power to do away with it and allow only the truth of God reside in your mind. Once you succeed in doing that you will see that you will crave God's presence more than anything else.

David is one man who greatly understood and enjoyed the benefits of being in God's presence continually. That is why he wrote in Psalm 42 vs 1 – 2:

[1]*As the hart panteth after the water brooks, so panteth my soul after thee, O God.*

² My soul thirseteth for God, for the living God: when shall I come and appear before God?

Verse one said, *Panteth*. To Pant as it appears here is a verb that means to long so eagerly for something. David longed eagerly for God's presence. It wasn't just a desire; it was a pant. He so inhabited the presence of God that he never lost any wars during his life time. God was always with him, guiding him through the toughest moments of his life, even when he sinned a great sin. That is why God finally referred to him as, *A man after my own heart.*

I can't stress this enough as a writer, but God eagerly seeks your fellowship. He is a merciful father and he wants to have a relationship with you, he wants to have you in his presence worshiping and communing with him. When you do all of these things, you get to experience God on a more personal level and trusting him becomes easy.

Remember all of the times God has been faithful

Why do we wake up each morning and expect to see the sun? Why do we look up and expect to see the sky? Why do we wake up each morning and expect to rise up on our feet and get to work? The answer to this is simply trust. We have built a level of trust in these things. Every single day of my life I have woken up to find the sun shining through my window, smiling and welcoming me to a lovely morning (except, of course, on cloudy rainy days. And even at that it is still somewhere behind the cloud.) Every morning of my life I have woken up to the sky still hanging more than 30,000fts above my head. Every morning I wake to my functional legs ready to take me through the day. It would be a real shock to wake up and find out that these things haven't functioned as they should, because my mind has been conditioned to remember all the times they never failed me.

I hope that analogy was powerful enough to paint a vivid picture in your mind.

Many times we find ourselves losing trust in God. Most times this happens because we have failed to sit back and think about all the times God has been faithful. The Devil is very good at taking away your gaze from God and placing it on your fears, making you ignore all of the times God has proven himself over and over.

The trick to getting ahead of this is to sit down quietly and ponder over God's faithfulness whenever you find yourself losing trust in God. One way to do this is to keep a gratitude journal where you write down all of the good things God has done for you.

<u>WHAT DO YOU DO WITH THIS?</u>

This is only the first volume of this book that explains the mystery of Psalm 91 and how you can enjoy all of God's promises embedded in this chapter.

The beauty of the scripture is that it has been given for our usage, a weapon we can use to wage war against the Devil. It is one thing to have the scripture and it is another thing to be able to use the scripture to outwit the Devil.

The Devil knows that he will be conquered if you ever have full access to God's word and understand how to use it. This is why you have to stay prepared and equipped by constantly studying the word of God and keeping it in your heart. God be with you.

***

If you enjoyed this book, I would love you to go over to Amazon and drop an honest review so that other people like you can see it. Your feedback means a lot to me as I research prayerfully and prepare the next book. Thank you very much.